Special Like Me...
Ehlers-Danlos Syndrome

Janelle Shannon H.C., LCSW,
and Founder of EDS-Kids

Special Like Me... Ehlers-Danlos Syndrome

Copyright © 2017 by Janelle Shannon H.C., LCSW,
and Founder of EDS-Kids

The content of this book is for general instruction only.
Each person's physical, emotional, and spiritual condition
is unique. The instruction in this book is not intended to replace or
interrupt the reader's relationship with a physician or other professional.
Please consult your doctor for matters pertaining to your specific health
and diet.

All rights reserved. No part of this publication may be reproduced,
distributed, or transmitted in any form or by any means, including
photocopying, recording, or
other electronic or mechanical methods, without prior written permission
of the publisher or author, except in
the case of brief quotations embodied in critical reviews
and certain other noncommercial uses permitted by copyright law. For
permission requests, email the author
at janelleshannonlcsw@gmail.com

To contact the publisher, visit
www.createspace.com
To contact the author, visit
Name: Janelle Shannon
E-mail: Janelleshannonlcsw@gmail.com
www.EDS-Kids.com
To contact the illustrator, visit
Name: Anngga Permana
E-mail: angga.edu04@gmail.com
Http://www.fiverr.com/asgard04

ISBN-13: 978-1542967785 - ISBN-10: 1542967783

Printed in the United States of America

# Dedication

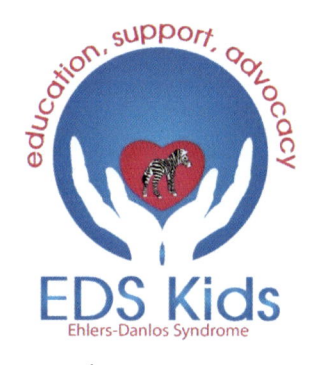

In 2011, I created EDS-Kids a Facebook group and page that provides individuals, families, and caregivers a safe place to unite and feel at home. I devote this book to our EDS-Kids community and all those who live with chronic illness and the people who lovingly care for them. I simply cannot begin to thank ALL OF YOU enough for being there and supporting us.

To my 15-year-old son William who helped to tell his story of living with EDS, my 16-year-old daughter Joyce-Marie who edited this book, to my beautiful daughters Domonique age 14 and Victoria age 12 who helped come up with ideas, encouraged each other and made this journey fun. To my husband and best friend Rick who has NEVER GIVEN UP no matter how hard things have been, who always finds time to show love, support, and most of all have fun.

# Introduction

This book is uniquely designed to assist parents, caregivers, and professionals facilitate conversations with children who have Ehlers-Danlos Syndrome (EDS). People with EDS have a genetic defect in their connective tissue, the tissue that provides support to many body parts such as the skin, bones, blood vessels, eyes, muscles, ligaments, and other organs. The symptoms vary from mildly loose joints to life-threatening complications. The fragile skin and unstable joints found in EDSers are the effects of faulty collagen (Sanders, n.d.).

Collagen is a protein, which behaves as a "glue" in the body, adding strength and elasticity to connective tissue. Collagen makes up 80% of our bodies. This diagnosis has no cure, comes with complications that are often unseen and can be life endangering. Diagnosis can take years, even lifetimes (The Ehlers-Danos Society, n.d.).

There are currently 6 major types of EDS and more being discovered. Every person with EDS has different symptoms and problems. Like a finger print, no two are alike, even among siblings.

This book is about a little boy's journey from bumps and bruises to diagnosis and beyond. The goal is to show EDSers and other children they are beautiful and amazing people that they can manage anything they set their mind to. Sometimes we must imagine outside the box and create new ways to do things i.e. playing sports and even writing at times. More than anything we want all EDSers to know they aren't alone. We want schools to understand each child is unique and need supports. Simply because you can't see it doesn't mean it's not real.

Special Like Me…
Ehlers-Danlos Syndrome

My name is William and I'm 5 years old. My parents and school teachers say i'm a klutz. I fall all the time and cause lots of bruises. I get tired easy and my body hurts all over.

**I LOVE FOOD!!**
I feel hungry all the time. My mom asks where I put it all. I tell her my tummy! I don't gain weight like other kids do. Mom reminds me to eat my fruits and vegtables and to drink lots of water so I can be healthy. Sometimes it's hard to stay healthy because my belly hurts so much that I get sick.

I get confused a lot because my head is foggy. I forget what I'm doing and need a lot of breaks. My doctors, teachers, and counselors don't recognize what is wrong with me. They say I'm wanting attention.

I was being silly and decided to curl up into a pretzel. My doctor couldn't believe it.

Mom took my photo and showed the doctor.

This doctor had me do silly movements and measured how far my fingers, arms, knees, and legs could bend.

It took 4 years to learn I have EDS.

Ehlers-Danlos Syndrome is a big word and I was scared. My mom hugged me tightly, told me I was not alone and she loved me.

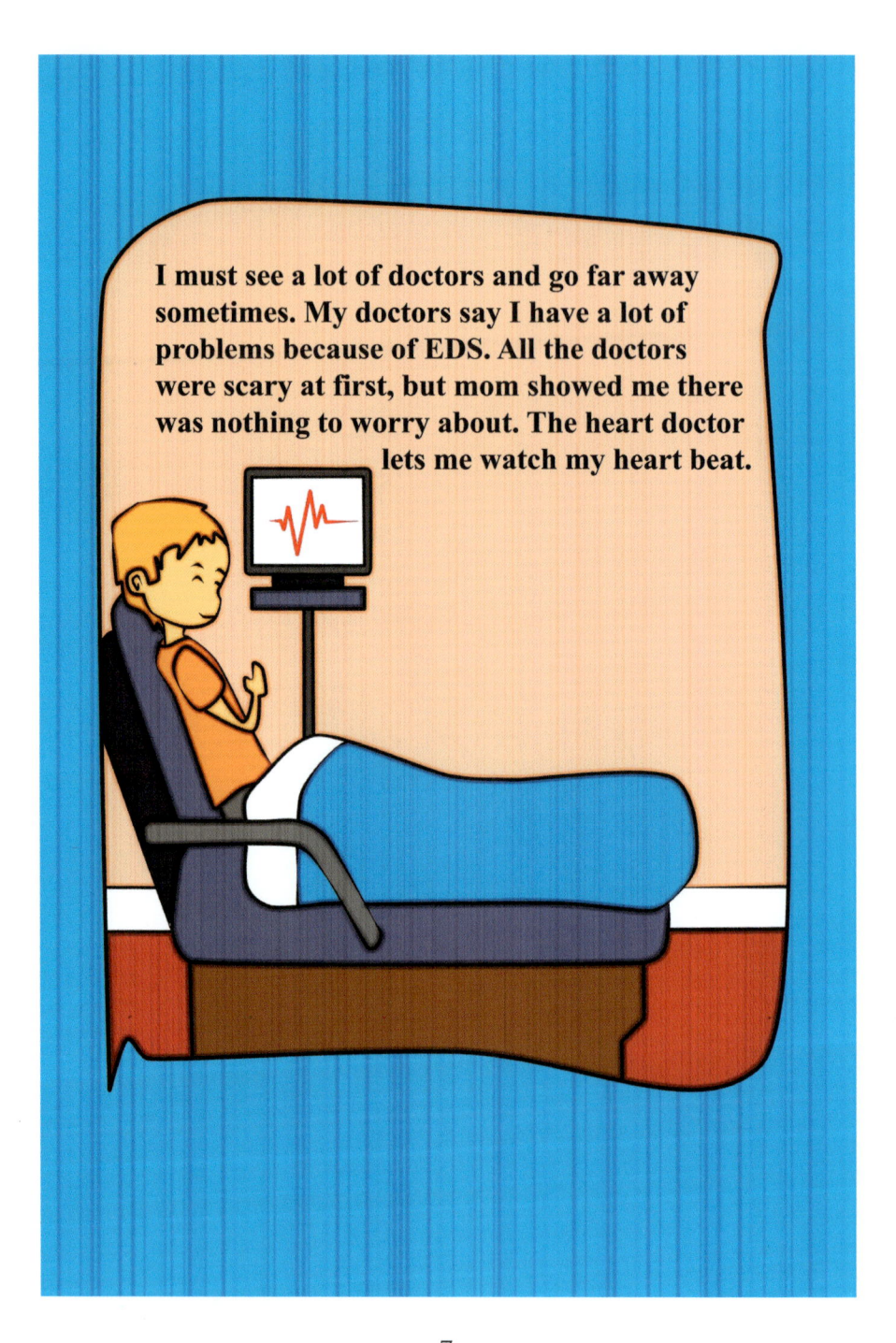

I must see a lot of doctors and go far away sometimes. My doctors say I have a lot of problems because of EDS. All the doctors were scary at first, but mom showed me there was nothing to worry about. The heart doctor lets me watch my heart beat.

I worry a lot and I get sad sometimes. My mom told me not to worry about what hasn't happened yet. If I worry too much I will feel sad all the time and miss the good things in my life.

I go to physical therapy to help me strengthen my body. Physical therapy is fun.

All my doctors say not to do silly things with my body.

I can break and pop all my bones out of where they are supposed to be very easy. This hurts me a lot!

**The doctor told me to stop playing soccer because it's dangerous for me. I have to find new ways to play games.**

**I learned to think about what I can do and not what I can't do.**

Sometimes I need my wheelchair because I am hurt or tired. The kids call me a faker and say I don't look

hurt or sick, mom says they just don't understand yet.

I have good teachers.
They help me tell my classmates about EDS.
Now I have lots of friends who I have fun with.

I have two little sisters who also have
EDS, we each have different problems and symptoms.

I want other kids with EDS to know they aren't alone, that they can be anything they want to be.

I'm happy being special like me!

# About the author

Janelle Shannon along with her husband adopted seven children. The three youngest siblings have Ehlers-Danlos Syndrome and other conditions. Janelle is a Licensed Mental Health Clinician, Board Certified Health Coach, Founder of EDS-Kids, and author. She received her training from the University of Southern California School of Social Work and Institute for Integrative Nutrition.

Janelle works with individuals, families, and couples. Specializing in health, mood, thinking disorders, and
chronic illness. Her primary focus has been assisting a variety of clients using a mindfulness, cognitive behavioral, and psychodynamic approach.  Clients describe her as "responsive", "inspiring" and "motivating." Janelle is available for readings, signings, and speak at bookstores, libraries, seminars, and other locations. For more information on Janelle or to stay in the know, visit https://www.EDS-KIDS.com.

# Credit

## About the Institute for Integrative Nutrition® (IIN)

This book was inspired by my experience at the Institute for Integrative Nutrition® (IIN) (Rosenthal, Launch Your Dream Book Course, n.d.), where I received my training in holistic wellness and health coaching. IIN offers a truly comprehensive Health Coach Training Program that invites students to deeply explore the things that are most nourishing to them. From the physical aspects of nutrition and eating wholesome foods that work best for each individual person, to the concept of Primary Food – the idea that everything in life, including our spirituality, career, relationships, and fitness contributes to our inner and outer health – IIN helped me reach optimal health and balance (Rosenthal, Intergrative Nutrition, n.d.). This inner journey unleashed the passion that compels me to share what I've learned and inspire others.

Beyond personal health, IIN offers training in health coaching, as well as business and marketing. Students who choose to pursue this field professionally complete the program equipped with the communication skills and branding knowledge they need to create a fulfilling career encouraging and supporting others in reaching their own health goals. From renowned wellness experts as Visiting Teachers to the convenience of their online learning platform, this school has changed my life, and I believe it will do the same for you. I invite you to learn more about the Institute for Integrative Nutrition and explore how the Health Coach Training Program can help you transform your life (Rosenthal, Intergrative Nutrition, n.d.). Feel free to contact me to hear more about my personal experience at or call (844) 315-8546 to learn more.

# Works Cited

Rosenthal, J. (n.d.). *Intergrative Nutrition.* Retrieved February 15, 2017, from Intergrative Nutrition: http://www.integrativenutrition.com/

Rosenthal, J. (n.d.). *Launch Your Dream Book Course.* Retrieved February 18, 2017, from Launch a Book, LLC: https://launchyourdreambook.com/

Sanders, L. (n.d.). *Ehlers-Danlos Syndrome Network C.A.R.E.S. Inc.* Retrieved from Ehlers Danlos Network : http://www.ehlersdanlosnetwork.org/

The Ehlers-Danos Society. (n.d.). *Ehlers-Danlos Info - Printable Materials.* Retrieved February 22, 2017, from The Ehlers-Danlos Society: http://ehlers-danlos.com/

# Resources

## Nutrition

http://www.integrativenutrition.com/

## Write a book

https://launchyourdreambook.com/

## EDS Information & Support

http://ehlers-danlos.com/
http://www.ehlersdanlosnetwork.org/
https://www.facebook.com/EDSForKids/
https://www.facebook.com/groups/edsforkids/

## Therapy

https://therapists.psychologytoday.com/309085
https://www.talkspace.com/room/Janelleshannon

Printed in Great Britain
by Amazon